Table of Cor

Greek-Style Chicken

6 boneless, skinless chicken thighs

½ teaspoon salt

½ teaspoon black pepper

1 tablespoon olive oil

½ cup chicken broth

1 lemon, thinly sliced

¼ cup pitted kalamata olives

1 clove garlic, minced

½ teaspoon dried oregano

Hot cooked orzo or rice

1. Remove visible fat from chicken; sprinkle chicken with salt and pepper. Heat oil in large skillet over medium-high heat. Brown chicken on all sides. Place in CROCK-POT® slow cooker.

2. Add broth, lemon, olives, garlic and oregano to CROCK-POT® slow cooker.

3. Cover; cook on LOW 5 to 6 hours or until chicken is tender. Serve with orzo.

MAKES 4 TO 6 SERVINGS

Turkey Breast with Barley-Cranberry Stuffing

2	cups reduced-sodium chicken broth
1	cup uncooked quick-cooking barley
½	cup chopped onion
½	cup dried cranberries
2	tablespoons slivered almonds, toasted*
½	teaspoon rubbed sage
½	teaspoon garlic-pepper seasoning
1	fresh or thawed frozen bone-in turkey breast half (about 2 pounds), skinned
⅓	cup finely chopped fresh parsley

To toast almonds, spread in single layer on baking sheet. Bake in preheated 350°F oven 8 to 10 minutes or until golden brown, stirring frequently.

1. Combine broth, barley, onion, cranberries, almonds, sage and garlic-pepper seasoning in **CROCK-POT®** slow cooker.

2. Coat large nonstick skillet with cooking spray. Heat over medium heat until hot. Brown turkey breast on all sides; add to **CROCK-POT®** slow cooker. Cover; cook on LOW 4 to 6 hours.

3. Transfer turkey to cutting board; cover with foil to keep warm. Let stand 10 to 15 minutes before carving. Stir parsley into stuffing in **CROCK-POT®** slow cooker. Slice turkey and serve with stuffing.

MAKES 6 SERVINGS

Tip: Browning poultry before cooking it in the **CROCK-POT®** slow cooker isn't necessary but helps to enhance the flavor and adds an oven-roasted appearance to the finished dish.

Simple Coq au Vin

4   chicken leg quarters

Salt and black pepper

2   tablespoons olive oil

8   ounces mushrooms, sliced

1   onion, cut into rings

½   cup red wine

½   teaspoon dried basil

½   teaspoon dried thyme

½   teaspoon dried oregano

Hot cooked rice

1. Sprinkle chicken with salt and pepper. Heat oil in large skillet over medium-high heat; brown chicken on all sides. Transfer chicken to **CROCK-POT**® slow cooker.

2. Cook and stir mushrooms and onion in same skillet 5 minutes or until tender. Add wine; stir and scrape brown bits from bottom of skillet. Add mixture to **CROCK-POT**® slow cooker. Sprinkle with basil, thyme and oregano. Cover; cook on LOW 8 to 10 hours or on HIGH 3 to 4 hours.

3. Serve over rice.

MAKES 4 SERVINGS

Cranberry-Barbecue Chicken Wings

3   pounds (about 27 wings) chicken wings
     Salt and black pepper
1   jar (12 ounces) cranberry-orange relish
½   cup barbecue sauce
2   tablespoons quick-cooking tapioca
1   tablespoon prepared mustard

1. Preheat broiler. Cut off chicken wing tips; discard. Cut each wing in half at joint. Place chicken on rack in broiler pan; season with salt and pepper.

2. Broil 4 to 5 inches from heat 10 to 12 minutes or until browned, turning once. Transfer chicken to **CROCK-POT®** slow cooker.

3. Stir relish, barbecue sauce, tapioca and mustard in small bowl. Pour over chicken. Cover; cook on LOW 4 to 5 hours.

MAKES ABOUT 16 APPETIZER SERVINGS OR 4 MAIN-DISH SERVINGS

For a meal: Serve one fourth of wings with rice for a main dish.

Tarragon Turkey & Pasta

1½	to 2 pounds turkey tenderloins
½	cup thinly sliced celery
¼	cup thinly sliced green onions
4	tablespoons minced fresh tarragon, divided
¼	cup dry white wine
1	teaspoon salt
1	teaspoon black pepper
½	cup plain yogurt
1	tablespoon minced fresh Italian parsley
1	tablespoon lemon juice
1½	tablespoons cornstarch
2	tablespoons water
4	cups pasta of your choice, cooked al dente

1. Combine turkey, celery, green onions, 2 tablespoons tarragon, wine, salt and pepper in **CROCK-POT®** slow cooker. Mix thoroughly. Cover; cook on LOW 6 to 8 hours or on HIGH 3½ to 4 hours or until turkey is no longer pink.

2. Remove turkey from **CROCK-POT®** slow cooker and cut into ½-inch-thick medallions. Set aside and keep warm. Turn **CROCK-POT®** slow cooker to HIGH. Stir in yogurt, remaining 2 tablespoons tarragon, parsley and lemon juice.

3. In small bowl, combine cornstarch and water. Add mixture to **CROCK-POT®** slow cooker and cook until sauce thickens. Serve turkey medallions over pasta. Drizzle with tarragon sauce.

MAKES 4 SERVINGS

Tip: For a 5, 6 or 7-quart **CROCK-POT®** slow cooker, double all ingredients.

Sweet Chicken Curry

- 1 pound boneless, skinless chicken breasts, cut into 1-inch pieces
- 1 large green or red bell pepper, cut into 1-inch pieces
- 1 large onion, sliced
- 1 large tomato, seeded and chopped
- ½ cup prepared mango chutney
- ¼ cup water
- 2 tablespoons cornstarch
- 1½ teaspoons curry powder
  Hot cooked rice

1. Place chicken, bell pepper and onion in **CROCK-POT®** slow cooker. Top with tomato.

2. Mix chutney, water, cornstarch and curry powder in small bowl. Pour over chicken.

3. Cover; cook on LOW 3½ to 4½ hours or until chicken is tender and no longer pink. Serve over rice.

MAKES 4 SERVINGS

Tuscan Pasta

1   pound boneless, skinless chicken breasts, cut into 1-inch pieces

2   cans (about 14 ounces each) Italian-style stewed tomatoes, undrained

1   can (about 15 ounces) red kidney beans, rinsed and drained

1   can (about 15 ounces) tomato sauce

1   cup water

1   jar (4½ ounces) sliced mushrooms, drained

1   medium green bell pepper, chopped

½   cup chopped onion

½   cup chopped celery

4   cloves garlic, minced

1   teaspoon Italian seasoning

6   ounces uncooked thin spaghetti, broken in half

1. Place all ingredients except spaghetti in CROCK-POT® slow cooker.

2. Cover; cook on LOW 4 hours or until vegetables are tender.

3. Stir in spaghetti. Cook on HIGH 10 minutes; stir. Cover; cook 35 minutes or until pasta is tender.

MAKES 8 SERVINGS

Chili Turkey Loaf

2 **pounds ground turkey**

1 **cup chopped onion**

⅔ **cup Italian-style seasoned dry bread crumbs**

½ **cup chopped green bell pepper**

½ **cup chili sauce**

2 **eggs, lightly beaten**

2 **tablespoons horseradish mustard**

4 **cloves garlic, minced**

1 **teaspoon salt**

½ **teaspoon Italian seasoning**

¼ **teaspoon black pepper**

Salsa (optional)

1. Make foil handles for loaf using technique described below. Mix all ingredients except salsa in large bowl. Shape into round loaf; place on foil strips. Transfer to bottom of **CROCK-POT**® slow cooker using foil handles.

2. Cover; cook on LOW 5 to 6 hours.

3. Remove loaf from **CROCK-POT**® slow cooker using foil handles. Let stand 5 minutes before serving. Cut into wedges and top with salsa, if desired.

MAKES 8 SERVINGS

Foil Handles: Tear off three 18×2-inch strips of heavy foil or use regular foil folded to double thickness. Crisscross foil strips in spoke design to place in bottom of CROCK-POT® slow cooker to allow for easy removal of turkey loaf.

Mu Shu Turkey

1   can (16 ounces) plums, drained and pitted

½   cup orange juice

¼   cup finely chopped onion

1   tablespoon minced fresh ginger

¼   teaspoon ground cinnamon

1   pound boneless turkey breast, cut into thin strips

6   (7-inch) flour tortillas

3   cups coleslaw mix

1. Place plums in blender or food processor. Cover; blend until almost smooth. Combine plums, orange juice, onion, ginger and cinnamon in CROCK-POT® slow cooker; mix well.

2. Place turkey over plum mixture. Cover; cook on LOW 3 to 4 hours.

3. Remove turkey from CROCK-POT® slow cooker. Divide evenly among tortillas. Spoon about 2 tablespoons plum sauce over turkey in each tortilla; top with about ½ cup coleslaw mix. Fold bottom edge of tortilla over filling; fold in sides. Roll up to completely enclose filling. Repeat with remaining tortillas. Use remaining plum sauce for dipping.

MAKES 6 SERVINGS

3-Cheese Chicken & Noodles

3	cups chopped cooked chicken
1½	cups cottage cheese
1	can (10¾ ounces) condensed cream of chicken soup, undiluted
1	package (8 ounces) wide egg noodles, cooked and drained
1	cup (4 ounces) shredded Monterey Jack cheese
½	cup grated Parmesan cheese
½	cup diced onion
½	cup diced celery
½	cup diced green bell pepper
½	cup diced red bell pepper
½	cup chicken broth
1	can (4 ounces) sliced mushrooms, drained
2	tablespoons butter, melted
½	teaspoon dried thyme

Combine all ingredients in CROCK-POT® slow cooker; mix well. Cover; cook on LOW 6 to 8 hours or on HIGH 3 to 4 hours.

MAKES 6 SERVINGS

Shredded Beef Fajitas

1   beef flank steak (about 1 pound)

1   can (14½ ounces) diced tomatoes with green chiles, undrained

1   cup chopped onion

½   medium green bell pepper, cut into ½-inch pieces

1   clove garlic, minced *or* ¼ teaspoon garlic powder

½   package (about 2 tablespoons) fajita seasoning mix

6   (8-inch) flour tortillas

   Toppings: reduced-fat sour cream, guacamole, shredded reduced-fat
      Cheddar cheese, salsa (optional)

1. Cut flank steak into 6 portions; place in CROCK-POT® slow cooker. Combine tomatoes with juice, onion, bell pepper, garlic and fajita seasoning mix in medium bowl. Pour over steak. Cover; cook on LOW 8 to 10 hours or on HIGH 4 to 5 hours or until beef is tender.

2. Remove beef; shred. Return beef to CROCK-POT® slow cooker and stir.

3. To serve fajitas, place meat mixture evenly into flour tortillas. Add toppings as desired; roll up tortillas.

MAKES 6 SERVINGS

Yankee Pot Roast and Vegetables

1 beef chuck pot roast (about 2½ pounds)

Salt and black pepper

3 unpeeled medium baking potatoes (about 1 pound), cut into quarters

2 large carrots, cut into ¾-inch slices

2 stalks celery, cut into ¾-inch slices

1 medium onion, sliced

1 large parsnip, cut into ¾-inch slices

2 bay leaves

1 teaspoon dried rosemary

½ teaspoon dried thyme

½ cup reduced-sodium beef broth

1. Trim excess fat from beef and discard. Cut beef into serving-size pieces; sprinkle with salt and pepper.

2. Combine potatoes, carrots, celery, onion, parsnip, bay leaves, rosemary and thyme in **CROCK-POT®** slow cooker. Place beef on top of vegetables. Pour broth over beef. Cover; cook on LOW 8½ to 9 hours or until beef is fork-tender.

3. Transfer beef to serving platter. Arrange vegetables around beef. Remove and discard bay leaves before serving.

MAKES 10 TO 12 SERVINGS

Tip: To make gravy, ladle cooking liquid into 2-cup measure; let stand 5 minutes. Skim off fat and discard. Measure remaining cooking liquid and heat to a boil in small saucepan. For each cup of cooking liquid, mix 2 tablespoons all-purpose flour with ¼ cup cold water until smooth. Stir flour mixture into boiling cooking liquid, stirring constantly 1 minute or until thickened.

Corned Beef and Cabbage

1   head cabbage (1½ pounds), cut into 6 wedges

4   ounces baby carrots

1   corned beef (3 pounds) with seasoning packet*

1   quart (4 cups) water

⅓   cup prepared mustard

⅓   cup honey

If seasoning packet is not perforated, poke several small holes with tip of paring knife.

1. Place cabbage in **CROCK-POT®** slow cooker; top with carrots. Place seasoning packet on top of vegetables. Place corned beef, fat side up, over seasoning packet and vegetables. Add water. Cover; cook on LOW 10 hours.

2. Combine mustard and honey in small bowl.

3. Discard seasoning packet. Slice beef and serve with vegetables and mustard sauce.

MAKES 6 SERVINGS

Broccoli and Beef Pasta

2 cups broccoli florets
   or 1 package (10 ounces) frozen broccoli, thawed

1 onion, thinly sliced

½ teaspoon dried basil

½ teaspoon dried oregano

½ teaspoon dried thyme

1 can (14½ ounces) Italian-style diced tomatoes, undrained

¾ cup beef broth

1 pound lean ground beef

2 cloves garlic, minced

2 cups cooked rotini pasta

¾ cup (3 ounces) shredded Cheddar cheese or grated Parmesan cheese, plus additional for garnish

2 tablespoons tomato paste

1. Layer broccoli, onion, basil, oregano, thyme, tomatoes with juice and broth in CROCK-POT® slow cooker. Cover; cook on LOW 2½ hours.

2. Cook and stir beef and garlic 6 to 8 minutes in large nonstick skillet over medium-high heat, stirring to break up meat. Drain fat. Transfer beef mixture to CROCK-POT® slow cooker. Cover; cook on LOW 2 hours.

3. Stir in pasta, cheese and tomato paste. Cover; cook 30 minutes or until cheese melts and mixture is heated through. Sprinkle with additional cheese as desired.

MAKES 4 SERVINGS

Swiss Steak

1   onion, sliced into thick rings

1   clove garlic, minced

1   beef round steak (about 2 pounds), cut into 8 pieces

    All-purpose flour

    Salt and black pepper

1   can (28 ounces) whole tomatoes, undrained

1   can (10¾ ounces) condensed tomato soup, undiluted

3   medium potatoes, unpeeled and diced

1   package (16 ounces) frozen peas and carrots

1   cup sliced celery

1. Place onion and garlic in **CROCK-POT®** slow cooker.

2. Dredge steak in flour seasoned with salt and pepper. Shake off excess flour. Place steak in **CROCK-POT®** slow cooker. Add tomatoes with juice. Cover with tomato soup. Add potatoes, peas and carrots and celery.

3. Cover; cook on LOW 6 to 8 hours or until meat and potatoes are tender.

MAKES 8 SERVINGS

Serving Suggestion: Try adding corn and beans. This recipe is very easy and definitely a family favorite!

BBQ Beef Sandwiches

1 boneless beef chuck roast (about 3 pounds)

¼ cup ketchup

2 tablespoons packed brown sugar

2 tablespoons red wine vinegar

1 tablespoon Dijon mustard

1 tablespoon Worcestershire sauce

1 clove garlic, minced

¼ teaspoon salt

¼ teaspoon liquid smoke (optional)

⅛ teaspoon black pepper

10 to 12 French rolls or sandwich buns

1. Place beef in **CROCK-POT®** slow cooker. Combine remaining ingredients except rolls in medium bowl; pour over meat.

2. Cover and cook on LOW 8 to 9 hours.

3. Remove beef from **CROCK-POT®** slow cooker; shred with 2 forks. Combine beef with 1 cup sauce from **CROCK-POT®** slow cooker. Evenly distribute meat and sauce mixture among warmed rolls.

MAKES 10 TO 12 SERVINGS

Hearty Chili Mac

1   pound 90% lean ground beef

1   can (14½ ounces) diced tomatoes, drained

1   cup chopped onion

1   tablespoon chili powder

1   clove garlic, minced

½   teaspoon salt

½   teaspoon ground cumin

½   teaspoon dried oregano

¼   teaspoon red pepper flakes

¼   teaspoon black pepper

2   cups cooked macaroni

1. Brown beef in large nonstick skillet over medium-high heat, stirring to break up meat. Drain fat and transfer beef to **CROCK-POT®** slow cooker. Add tomatoes, onion, chili powder, garlic, salt, cumin, oregano, red pepper flakes and black pepper; mix well.

2. Cover; cook on LOW 4 hours.

3. Stir in macaroni. Cover; cook 1 hour.

MAKES 4 SERVINGS

Steak San Marino

¼ cup all-purpose flour

1 teaspoon salt

½ teaspoon black pepper

1 beef round steak (about 1½ pounds), cut into 4 pieces *or* 2 beef top round steaks, cut in half

1 can (8 ounces) tomato sauce

2 carrots, chopped

½ onion, chopped

1 stalk celery, chopped

1 teaspoon Italian seasoning

½ teaspoon Worcestershire sauce

1 bay leaf

Hot cooked rice

1. Combine flour, salt and pepper in small bowl. Dredge each piece of beef in flour mixture; place in **CROCK-POT®** slow cooker. Combine tomato sauce, carrots, onion, celery, Italian seasoning, Worcestershire sauce and bay leaf in small bowl; pour over beef. Cover; cook on LOW 8 to 10 hours or on HIGH 4 to 5 hours.

2. Remove and discard bay leaf. Serve steaks and sauce over rice.

MAKES 4 SERVINGS

Pork and Mushroom Ragoût

Nonstick cooking spray

1   boneless pork loin roast (1¼ pounds)

1¼   cups canned crushed tomatoes, divided

2   tablespoons cornstarch

2   teaspoons dried savory

3   sun-dried tomatoes, chopped

1   package (8 ounces) sliced fresh mushrooms

1   large onion, sliced

1   teaspoon black pepper

3   cups hot cooked noodles

1. Spray large nonstick skillet with cooking spray; heat over medium heat until hot. Brown roast on all sides; set aside.

2. Combine ½ cup crushed tomatoes, cornstarch, savory and sun-dried tomatoes in **CROCK-POT®** slow cooker; mix well. Layer mushrooms, onion and pork over tomato mixture.

3. Pour remaining ¾ cup crushed tomatoes over pork; sprinkle with pepper. Cover; cook on LOW 4 to 6 hours or until internal temperature of pork reaches 165°F when tested with meat thermometer inserted into thickest part of roast.

4. Transfer roast to cutting board; tent with foil. Let stand 10 to 15 minutes. (Internal temperature will continue to rise 5° to 10°F during stand time.) Slice roast. Serve with sauce over hot cooked noodles.

MAKES 6 SERVINGS

Cajun-Style Country Ribs

- 2 cups baby carrots
- 1 large onion, coarsely chopped
- 1 large green bell pepper, cut into 1-inch pieces
- 1 large red bell pepper, cut into 1-inch pieces
- 2 teaspoons minced garlic
- 2 tablespoons Cajun or Creole seasoning, divided
- 3½ to 4 pounds country-style pork ribs
- 1 can (about 14 ounces) stewed tomatoes, undrained
- 2 tablespoons water
- 1 tablespoon cornstarch

  Hot cooked rice

1. Combine carrots, onion, bell peppers, garlic and 2 teaspoons Cajun seasoning in **CROCK-POT**® slow cooker; mix well.

2. Trim excess fat from ribs. Cut into individual ribs. Sprinkle 1 tablespoon Cajun seasoning over ribs; place in **CROCK-POT**® slow cooker over vegetables. Pour tomatoes with juice over ribs. Cover; cook on LOW 6 to 8 hours or until ribs are fork tender.

3. Remove ribs and vegetables from cooking liquid to serving platter. Let liquid stand 5 minutes to allow fat to rise. Skim off fat. In small bowl, blend water, cornstarch and remaining 1 teaspoon Cajun seasoning until smooth. Stir into **CROCK-POT**® slow cooker. Cook, uncovered, on HIGH 15 to 30 minutes or until sauce is thickened. Return ribs and vegetables to sauce; carefully stir to coat. Serve with rice.

MAKES 6 TO 8 SERVINGS

Shredded Pork Wraps

1   **cup salsa, divided**

2   **tablespoons cornstarch**

1   **boneless pork loin roast (2 pounds)**

6   **(8-inch) flour tortillas**

3   **cups broccoli slaw mix**

½   **cup (2 ounces) shredded Cheddar cheese**

1. Combine ¼ cup salsa and cornstarch in small bowl; stir until smooth. Pour mixture into **CROCK-POT®** slow cooker. Top with pork roast. Pour remaining ¾ cup salsa over roast. Cover; cook on LOW 6 to 8 hours.

2. Transfer roast to cutting board. Trim and discard fat from pork. Pull pork into coarse shreds using 2 forks.

3. Divide shredded meat evenly among tortillas. Spoon about 2 tablespoons salsa mixture on top of meat in each tortilla. Top evenly with broccoli slaw and cheese. Fold bottom edge of tortilla over filling; fold in sides. Roll up completely to enclose filling. Serve remaining salsa mixture as dipping sauce.

Vegetable-Stuffed Pork Chops

4	double pork loin chops, well trimmed
	Salt and black pepper
1	can (about 15 ounces) corn, drained
1	green bell pepper, chopped
1	cup Italian-style seasoned dry bread crumbs
1	small onion, chopped
½	cup uncooked long-grain converted rice
1	can (8 ounces) tomato sauce

1. Cut pocket into each pork chop. Lightly season pockets with salt and black pepper. Combine corn, bell pepper, bread crumbs, onion and rice in large bowl. Stuff pork chops with rice mixture. Secure along fat side with toothpicks.

2. Place remaining rice mixture in **CROCK-POT®** slow cooker. Place stuffed pork chops on top. Coat top of each pork chop with tomato sauce. Pour any remaining tomato sauce over top. Cover; cook on LOW 8 to 10 hours.

3. Remove pork chops to serving platter. Remove and discard toothpicks. Serve pork chops with rice mixture.

MAKES 4 SERVINGS

Sweet and Sour Spareribs

4	pounds pork spareribs
1⅓	cups chicken broth
1	cup dry sherry or chicken broth
½	cup pineapple, mango or guava juice
2	tablespoons packed brown sugar
2	tablespoons cider vinegar
2	tablespoons soy sauce
1	clove garlic, minced
½	teaspoon salt
¼	teaspoon black pepper
⅛	teaspoon red pepper flakes
2	tablespoons cornstarch
¼	cup water

1. Preheat oven to 400°F. Place ribs in foil-lined shallow roasting pan. Bake 30 minutes, turning after 15 minutes. Remove from oven. Cut meat into 2-rib portions. Place ribs in **CROCK-POT®** slow cooker. Add remaining ingredients, except cornstarch and water. Cover; cook on LOW 6 hours or until ribs are tender.

2. Transfer ribs to platter; keep warm. Let liquid in **CROCK-POT®** slow cooker stand 5 minutes to allow fat to rise. Skim off fat.

3. Blend cornstarch and water until smooth. Stir mixture into **CROCK-POT®** slow cooker; mix well. Cook, uncovered, on HIGH 15 minutes or until slightly thickened.

MAKES 4 SERVINGS

Cheesy Pork and Potatoes

½   pound ground pork, cooked and crumbled

½   cup finely crushed saltine crackers

⅓   cup barbecue sauce

1   egg

3   tablespoons butter or margarine

1   tablespoon vegetable oil

4   potatoes, peeled and thinly sliced

1   onion, thinly sliced

1   cup (4 ounces) shredded
      mozzarella cheese

⅔   cup evaporated milk

1   teaspoon salt

¼   teaspoon paprika

⅛   teaspoon black pepper

    Chopped fresh parsley (optional)

1. Combine pork, crackers, barbecue sauce and egg in large bowl; shape mixture into 6 patties.

2. Heat butter and oil in medium skillet. Cook and stir potatoes and onion until lightly browned; drain. Place in **CROCK-POT®** slow cooker.

3. Combine cheese, milk, salt, paprika and pepper in small bowl. Pour mixture into **CROCK-POT®** slow cooker. Layer pork patties on top.

4. Cover; cook on LOW 3 to 5 hours. Garnish with parsley. Serve with vegetable side, if desired.

MAKES 6 SERVINGS

Beef Stew with Bacon, Onion and Sweet Potatoes

1   pound beef stew meat, cut into 1-inch chunks

1   can (14½ ounces) beef broth

2   medium sweet potatoes, peeled and cut into 2-inch pieces*

1   large onion, cut into 1½-inch pieces

2   slices thick-cut bacon, diced

1   teaspoon dried thyme

1   teaspoon salt

¼   teaspoon black pepper

2   tablespoons cornstarch

2   tablespoons water

*You may substitute 12 to 13 ounces carrots or white potatoes, cut into 2-inch chunks.

1. Coat CROCK-POT® slow cooker with nonstick cooking spray. Add beef, broth, potatoes, onion, bacon, thyme, salt and pepper; stir to combine. Cover; cook on LOW 7 to 8 hours or on HIGH 4 to 5 hours.

2. Transfer beef and vegetables to serving bowl with slotted spoon; keep warm.

3. Turn to HIGH. Combine cornstarch and water in small bowl until smooth. Stir into juices in CROCK-POT® slow cooker. Cook, uncovered, 15 minutes or until thickened, stirring occasionally. Stir in beef and vegetables. Cover and cook 15 minutes or until warm.

MAKES 4 SERVINGS

Chicken and Vegetable Chowder

1 pound boneless, skinless chicken breasts, cut into 1-inch pieces

1 can (14½ ounces) reduced-sodium chicken broth

1 can (10¾ ounces) condensed cream of potato soup, undiluted

1 package (10 ounces) frozen broccoli florets, thawed

1 cup sliced carrots

1 jar (4½ ounces) sliced mushrooms, drained

½ cup chopped onion

½ cup whole kernel corn

2 cloves garlic, minced

½ teaspoon dried thyme leaves

⅓ cup half-and-half

1. Combine chicken, broth, soup, broccoli, carrots, mushrooms, onion, corn, garlic and thyme in CROCK-POT® slow cooker; mix well.

2. Cover; cook on LOW 5 to 6 hours.

3. Stir in half-and-half. Cover; cook on HIGH 15 minutes or until heated through.

MAKES 6 SERVINGS

Variation: Add ½ cup (2 ounces) shredded Swiss or Cheddar cheese just before serving, stirring over LOW heat until melted.

Savory Pea Soup with Sausage

8   ounces smoked sausage, cut lengthwise into halves, then cut into ½-inch pieces

3   medium carrots, sliced

1   package (16 ounces) dried split peas, rinsed and sorted

2   stalks celery, sliced

1   medium onion, chopped

¾   teaspoon dried marjoram leaves

1   bay leaf

2   cans (14½ ounces each) reduced-sodium chicken broth

1. Heat medium nonstick skillet over medium heat. Add sausage; cook 5 to 8 minutes or until browned. Drain fat. Combine sausage, carrots, peas, celery, onion, marjoram and bay leaf in **CROCK-POT®** slow cooker. Pour broth over mixture.

2. Cover; cook on LOW 4 to 5 hours or until peas are tender. Remove and discard bay leaf. Cover; let stand 15 minutes to thicken.

MAKES 6 SERVINGS

Italian Beef and Barley Soup

1 boneless beef top sirloin steak (about 1½ pounds)

1 tablespoon vegetable oil

4 medium carrots or parsnips, cut into ¼-inch slices

1 cup chopped onion

1 teaspoon dried thyme

½ teaspoon dried rosemary

¼ teaspoon black pepper

⅓ cup uncooked pearl barley

2 cans (14½ ounces each) beef broth

1 can (about 14 ounces) diced tomatoes with Italian seasoning, undrained

1. Cut beef into 1-inch pieces. Heat oil over medium-high heat in large skillet. Brown beef on all sides; set aside.

2. Place carrots and onion in CROCK-POT® slow cooker; sprinkle with thyme, rosemary and pepper. Top with barley and beef. Pour broth and tomatoes with juice over meat.

3. Cover; cook on LOW 8 to 10 hours or until beef is tender.

MAKES 6 SERVINGS

Tip: Choose pearl barley rather than quick-cooking barley, because it will stand up to long cooking.

Navy Bean Bacon Chowder

1½ cups dried navy beans, rinsed and sorted

2 cups cold water

6 slices thick-cut bacon

1 medium carrot, cut lengthwise into halves, then cut into 1-inch pieces

1 small turnip, cut into 1-inch pieces

1 stalk celery, chopped

1 medium onion, chopped

1 teaspoon Italian seasoning

⅛ teaspoon black pepper

1 can (46 ounces) reduced-sodium chicken broth

1 cup milk

1. Soak beans overnight in cold water; drain.

2. Cook bacon in medium skillet over medium heat. Drain fat; crumble bacon. Combine beans, bacon, carrot, turnip, celery, onion, Italian seasoning and pepper in **CROCK-POT®** slow cooker. Add broth. Cover; cook on LOW 8 to 9 hours or until beans are tender.

3. Ladle 2 cups of soup mixture into food processor or blender. Process until smooth; return to **CROCK-POT®** slow cooker. Add milk. Cover; cook on HIGH 15 minutes or until heated through.

MAKES 6 SERVINGS

Chicken and Wild Rice Soup

- 3 cans (14½ ounces each) chicken broth
- 1 pound boneless, skinless chicken breasts or thighs, cut into bite-size pieces
- 2 cups water
- 1 cup sliced celery
- 1 cup diced carrots
- 1 package (6 ounces) converted long grain and wild rice mix with seasoning packet (not quick-cooking or instant rice)
- ½ cup chopped onion
- ½ teaspoon black pepper
- 2 teaspoons white vinegar (optional)
- 1 tablespoon dried parsley flakes

1. In CROCK-POT® slow cooker, combine broth, chicken, water, celery, carrots, rice and seasoning packet, onion and pepper; mix well.

2. Cover; cook on LOW 6 to 7 hours or on HIGH 4 to 5 hours or until chicken is tender.

3. Stir in vinegar, if desired. Sprinkle with parsley.

MAKES 9 SERVINGS

Rustic Potatoes au Gratin

½ cup milk

1 can (10¾ ounces) condensed Cheddar cheese soup, undiluted

1 package (8 ounces) cream cheese, softened

1 clove garlic, minced

¼ teaspoon ground nutmeg

⅛ teaspoon black pepper

2 pounds baking potatoes, cut into ¼-inch slices

1 small onion, thinly sliced

   Paprika (optional)

1. Heat milk in small saucepan over medium heat until small bubbles form around edge. Remove from heat. Add soup, cream cheese, garlic, nutmeg and pepper. Stir until smooth.

2. Layer one fourth of potatoes and one fourth of onion in **CROCK-POT®** slow cooker. Top with one fourth of soup mixture. Repeat layers 3 times, using remaining potatoes, onion and soup mixture.

3. Cover; cook on LOW 6½ to 7 hours or until potatoes are tender and most of liquid is absorbed. Sprinkle with paprika.

MAKES 6 SERVINGS

Cheesy Broccoli Casserole

2   packages (10 ounces each) frozen chopped broccoli, thawed

1   can (10¾ ounces) condensed cream of potato soup

1¼ cups (5 ounces) shredded sharp Cheddar cheese, divided

¼   cup minced onion

1   teaspoon hot pepper sauce

1   cup crushed potato chips or saltine crackers

1. Lightly grease **CROCK-POT®** slow cooker. Add broccoli, soup, 1 cup cheese, onion and pepper sauce; mix well.

2. Cover; cook on LOW 5 to 6 hours or on HIGH 2½ to 3 hours.

3. Sprinkle chips and remaining ¼ cup cheese over broccoli mixture. Cook, uncovered, on LOW 30 to 60 minutes or until cheese melts.

MAKES 4 TO 6 SERVINGS

Note: For a crispier topping, after step 2, transfer casserole to a baking dish. Sprinkle with remaining cheese and crackers. Bake 10 to 15 minutes in preheated 400°F oven.

Spinach Gorgonzola Corn Bread

2 boxes (8½ ounces each) cornbread mix

3 eggs

½ cup cream

1 box (10 ounces) frozen chopped spinach, thawed and drained

1 cup (4 ounces) crumbled Gorgonzola

1 teaspoon black pepper

Paprika (optional)

1. Coat 1½- to 2-quart CROCK-POT® slow cooker with nonstick cooking spray.

2. Mix all ingredients in medium bowl. Place batter in CROCK-POT® slow cooker. Cover; cook on HIGH 1½ hours. Sprinkle with paprika for more colorful crust, if desired. Let bread cool completely before inverting onto serving platter.

MAKES 10 TO 12 SERVINGS

Note: Cook only on HIGH setting for proper crust and texture.

Risi Bisi

1½ cups uncooked converted long-grain rice

¾ cup chopped onion

2 cloves garlic, minced

2 cans (14½ ounces each) reduced-sodium chicken broth

⅓ cup water

¾ teaspoon Italian seasoning

½ teaspoon dried basil

½ cup frozen peas

¼ cup grated Parmesan cheese

¼ cup toasted pine nuts (optional)

1. Combine rice, onion and garlic in CROCK-POT® slow cooker.

2. Bring broth and water to a boil in small saucepan. Stir broth mixture, Italian seasoning and basil into rice mixture. Cover; cook on LOW 2 to 3 hours or until liquid is absorbed.

3. Add peas. Cover; cook on LOW 1 hour. Stir in cheese. Sprinkle with pine nuts, if desired.

MAKES 6 SERVINGS

Orange Spice-Glazed Carrots

1   package (32 ounces) baby carrots

½   cup packed light brown sugar

½   cup orange juice

3   tablespoons butter or margarine

¾   teaspoon ground cinnamon

¼   teaspoon ground nutmeg

¼   cup cold water

2   tablespoons cornstarch

1. Combine carrots, brown sugar, juice, butter, cinnamon and nutmeg in 1½- to 3-quart **CROCK-POT®** slow cooker. Cover; cook on LOW 3½ to 4 hours or until carrots are crisp-tender.

2. Spoon carrots into serving bowl. Transfer juices to small saucepan; heat to a boil.

3. Mix water and cornstarch in cup or small bowl until smooth; stir into saucepan. Boil 1 minute or until thickened, stirring constantly. Spoon over carrots.

MAKES 6 SERVINGS

Homestyle Apple Brown Betty

6   cups of your favorite cooking apples, peeled, cored and cut into eighths

1   cup bread crumbs

1   teaspoon ground cinnamon

1   teaspoon ground nutmeg

⅛   teaspoon salt

¾   cup packed brown sugar

½   cup (1 stick) butter or margarine, melted

¼   cup finely chopped walnuts

1. Lightly grease 2½- to 3-quart CROCK-POT® slow cooker; place apples on bottom.

2. Combine bread crumbs, cinnamon, nutmeg, salt, brown sugar, butter and walnuts, and spread over apples.

3. Cover; cook on LOW 3 to 4 hours or on HIGH 2 hours.

MAKES 8 SERVINGS

Tip: For a 5, 6 or 7-quart CROCK-POT® slow cooker, double all ingredients.

Luscious Pecan Bread Pudding

3	cups day-old French bread cubes
3	tablespoons chopped pecans, toasted
2¼	cups low-fat (1%) milk
2	eggs, beaten
½	cup granulated sugar
1	teaspoon vanilla
¾	teaspoon ground cinnamon, divided
¾	cup reduced-calorie cranberry juice cocktail
1½	cups frozen pitted tart cherries
2	tablespoons sugar substitute

1. Toss bread cubes and pecans in soufflé dish. Combine milk, eggs, sugar, vanilla and ½ teaspoon cinnamon in large bowl. Pour over bread mixture in soufflé dish. Cover tightly with foil. Make foil handles (see note). Place soufflé dish in 2½- to 4-quart **CROCK-POT®** slow cooker. Pour hot water into slow cooker to about 1½ inches from top of soufflé dish. Cover; cook on LOW 2 to 3 hours.

2. Meanwhile, combine cranberry juice and remaining ¼ teaspoon cinnamon in small saucepan; stir in frozen cherries. Bring sauce to a boil over medium heat; cook about 5 minutes. Remove from heat. Stir in sugar substitute.

3. Lift soufflé dish from **CROCK-POT®** slow cooker with foil handles. Serve bread pudding with cherry sauce.

MAKES 6 SERVINGS

Foil Handles: Tear off three 18×2-inch strips of heavy foil or use regular foil folded to double thickness. Crisscross foil strips in spoke design and place in **CROCK-POT®** slow cooker to allow for easy removal of soufflé dish.

Brownie Bottoms

½ cup packed brown sugar

¾ cup water

2 tablespoons unsweetened cocoa powder

2½ cups packaged brownie mix

1 package (2¾ ounces) instant chocolate pudding mix

½ cup milk chocolate chips

2 eggs, beaten

3 tablespoons butter or margarine, melted

1. Lightly spray 4-quart **CROCK-POT®** slow cooker with nonstick cooking spray. In small saucepan, combine brown sugar, water and cocoa powder; bring to a boil.

2. Combine brownie mix, pudding mix, chocolate chips, eggs and butter in medium bowl; stir until well blended. Spread batter into CROCK-POT® slow cooker; pour boiling sugar mixture over batter. Cover; cook on HIGH 1½ hours.

3. Turn off heat and let stand 30 minutes. Serve warm.

MAKES 6 SERVINGS

Note: Serve this warm chocolate dessert with whipped cream or ice cream.

Tip: For a 5, 6 or 7-quart CROCK-POT® slow cooker, you may double all ingredients.

Fruit & Nut Baked Apples

4   large baking apples, such as Rome Beauty or Jonathan

1   tablespoon lemon juice

⅓   cup chopped dried apricots

⅓   cup chopped walnuts or pecans

3   tablespoons packed light brown sugar

½   teaspoon ground cinnamon

2   tablespoons melted butter or margarine

    Caramel ice cream topping (optional)

1. Scoop out center of each apple, leaving 1½-inch-wide cavity about ½ inch from bottom. Peel top of apple down about 1 inch. Brush peeled edges evenly with lemon juice. Mix apricots, walnuts, brown sugar and cinnamon in small bowl. Add butter; mix well. Spoon mixture evenly into apple cavities.

2. Pour ½ cup water in bottom of 4- to 7-quart CROCK-POT® slow cooker. Place 2 apples in water. Arrange remaining 2 apples above but not directly on top of bottom apples.

3. Cover; cook on LOW 3 to 4 hours or until apples are tender. Serve warm or at room temperature with caramel ice cream topping, if desired.

MAKES 4 SERVINGS

Decadent Chocolate Delight

1 package (18¼ ounces) chocolate cake mix

1 cup (8 ounces) sour cream

1 cup semisweet chocolate chips

1 cup water

4 eggs

¾ cup vegetable oil

1 package (4-serving size) chocolate instant pudding and pie filling mix

Vanilla ice cream

1. Coat 4- to 5-quart CROCK-POT® slow cooker with butter or nonstick cooking spray.

2. Combine all ingredients, except ice cream, in medium bowl; mix well. Transfer to CROCK-POT® slow cooker.

3. Cover; cook on LOW 6 to 8 hours or on HIGH 3 to 4 hours. Serve hot or warm with ice cream.

MAKES 12 SERVINGS

Spiced Apple & Cranberry Compote

2½   cups cranberry juice cocktail

1   package (6 ounces) dried apples

½   cup (2 ounces) dried cranberries

½   cup Rhine wine or apple juice

½   cup honey

2   cinnamon sticks, broken into halves

Frozen yogurt or ice cream (optional)

Additional cinnamon sticks (optional)

1. Mix juice, apples, cranberries, wine, honey and cinnamon stick halves in 2- to 3-quart CROCK-POT® slow cooker. Cover and cook on LOW 4 to 5 hours or until liquid is absorbed and fruit is tender.

2. Remove and discard cinnamon stick halves. Ladle compote into bowls. Serve warm, at room temperature or chilled with scoop of frozen yogurt or ice cream, if desired. Garnish with additional cinnamon sticks, if desired.

MAKES 6 SERVINGS

Coconut Rice Pudding

2 cups water

1 cup uncooked
    converted long
    grain rice

1 tablespoon unsalted
    butter

Pinch salt

2¼ cups evaporated milk

1 can (14 ounces)
    cream of coconut

½ cup golden raisins

3 egg yolks, beaten

Grated peel of 2 limes

1 teaspoon vanilla

Toasted shredded
    coconut (optional)

1. Spray 3- to 5-quart **CROCK-POT**® slow cooker with nonstick cooking spray. Place water, rice, butter and salt in medium saucepan. Bring to a boil over high heat, stirring frequently. Reduce heat to low. Cover; cook 10 to 12 minutes. Remove from heat. Let stand covered 5 minutes.

2. Add evaporated milk, cream of coconut, raisins, egg yolks, lime peel and vanilla; mix well. Add rice; stir until blended. Pour into prepared **CROCK-POT**® slow cooker.

3. Cover; cook on LOW 4 hours or on HIGH 2 hours. Stir every 30 minutes, if possible. Pudding will thicken as it cools. Garnish with toasted shredded coconut, if desired.

MAKES 6 SERVINGS

Triple Chocolate Fantasy

2   **pounds white almond bark, broken into pieces**

1   **bar (4 ounces) sweetened chocolate, broken into pieces***

1   **package (12 ounces) semisweet chocolate chips**

3   **cups coarsely chopped pecans, lightly toasted**

*Use your favorite high-quality chocolate candy bar

1. Place bark, sweetened chocolate and chocolate chips in 2- to 4-quart **CROCK-POT®** slow cooker. Cover; cook on HIGH 1 hour. Do not stir.

2. Turn **CROCK-POT®** slow cooker to LOW. Continue cooking 1 hour, stirring every 15 minutes. Stir in nuts.

3. Drop mixture by tablespoonfuls onto baking sheet covered with waxed paper; let cool. Store in tightly covered container.

MAKES 36 PIECES

Variations: Instead of pecans, try crushed peppermint candy, candy-coated baking bits, crushed toffee, peanuts or pistachios, chopped gum drops, chopped dried fruit, candied cherries, chopped marshmallows or sweetened coconut.